Inspired
To
Victory

Debbie Taylor

ISBN:1505344107
ISBN-13:9781505344103

ACKNOWLEDGMENTS

I thank my God Who sent Jesus to become sin for me that I might be made the righteousness of God in Christ and have bold access to God's throne of grace.

Many thanks to Stacy Pearson for her

invaluable input in making this book a reality.

Romans 10: 9, 10

Vs 9: If you confess with your mouth

The Lord Jesus and

Believe in your heart that God has

Raised Him from the dead, you

Will be saved.

Vs 10: For with the heart one believes

Unto righteousness, and with the

Mouth confession is made

Unto salvation

CONTENTS

JESUS LOVES YOU

Jesus loves you so very much.

He's ready to help with a loving touch.

He leads in the way He wants you to go. [1]

So follow Him closely and His blessings will show.

Never forget to be thankful at heart.

This is how a new life you can start.

Give your heart to the Lord, Give no place to the devil[2]

Jesus will guide you and make your path level.

Always acknowledge the goodness of God.

A pathway to heaven is where you will trod.

Leave all of your worries, your cares and your strife

At the cross of Jesus. Then, take up His life.

Debbie Taylor

Put on His righteousness, His joy and His peace

By the words of your mouth, drive out unbelief

Believe in your heart and confess with your mouth

From your innermost being, God's Life will pour out.[3]

That is how in this world Christ will be known

As you walk out each day with God's love overflowin'.

Walk in the Spirit, walk not in the flesh,[4]

You'll please the Father and you'll pass the test.

On that day soon to come, it's not far away.

When you stand face to face, you'll hear Father say[5]

"You've finished the course. You've run a good race

It's time to come home, now come take your place."[6]

Debbie Taylor

TRUST IN HIS WORD

You're mighty to deliver. You're mighty and true.

I trust in Your Word, Lord, now I rest in You.[7]

You're just and You're holy, You're righteous & strong.

All You do, Father, is right, and not wrong.

You're mighty to deliver. Yes, mighty and strong

You see where I am and You help me along.

There's nothing too hard, nothing I cannot do.[8]

Because You're by my side, I put my trust in You.

The path that I trod grows brighter each day.

I don't do my will, but I do it Your way.

I'm blesssed going in and I'm blessed going out.[9]

I'm happy and free as I walk about.

Debbie Taylor

I sing to my King 'cause He's coming again.[10]

I do all His will and that keeps me from sin.

I'm a victorious child in this earth here below.

Because of His glory & grace in my life now does grow.

Many will see Him by the love that I show.

They'll make Jesus their Lord with gifts to bestow.

Many souls in the Kingdom, turned from darkness to light

because I did trust Him... I did what was right.

From this day forth you can do the same.

Obey God's Word, with His grace you can reign.[11]

You are the one with authority now.[12]

Trust in His Word and He'll show you how.

Debbie Taylor

RECEIVE THE VICTORY

Jesus is the mighty Rock.

He loves each member of His flock.

Each hair of your head He has counted.[13]

But, the battle call has been sounded.

When troubles come and storm winds blow,

Jesus is the place to go.

The devil calls with a crafty roar,

But wait, see what God has in store.

The desire of the righteous shall be granted.[14]

Your foot will not be supplanted.

God will hear you as you call.[15]

He will uphold you lest you fall.[16]

Debbie Taylor

"The battle is mine," thus says the Lord.

"You must stand on My two edged sword."

The victory was won by God's own Son.

From the beginning of time, the battle was won.

Today may be your opportunity,

To in the Word, make scrutiny.

God has a promise and a plan.

Receive the victory, from God's own hand.[17]

Debbie Taylor

REDEMPTION

God had a plan to redeem to Himself[18]

The things that sin had put on the shelf.

He sent His Son to redeem back His man

The Last Adam, Jesus, the Spotless Lamb.[19]

The devil had brought us such dark oppressions

He stole from us all of our valued possessions.[20]

Jesus has freed us from his awful hold.

Now satan must pay us all back sevenfold.[21]

We were living each day very fearful.

Then a preacher came preaching an earful.[22]

A Word of love and repentance he brought us

In our hearts a deliverance it wrought us.

Debbie Taylor

By the Word we received, faith has grown.[23]

Signs and wonders by faith have been shown.[24]

Grace and mercy have followed, we've learned

The Word of God, when from sin we have turned.

We've confessed Jesus as Lord & made our hearts pure.[25]

The Lord has forgiven and cleansed us we're sure.[26]

We've opened our lips and new praises we've sung.

Our lives in the arms of the Lord we have flung.

Our life is now hid with Christ in God[27]

Our feet with the Gospel of Peace now are shod.

It's by His love in our spirits He's master[28]

He perfects us through the gift of the pastor.[29]

Debbie Taylor

We submit to His Word in willing delight.

The darkness is gone now because of the Light.[30]

He's the Light of the World and He shines in our hearts

By the new birth He's given us new spiritual parts.[31]

Now we are the ones who boldly proclaim

The Gospel with power that breaks every chain.[32]

If you are still living in darkness and fear

You must hear the good news with ears that will hear.

We go forth believing; we lay hands on the sick.[33]

All those hard hearts, the Gospel will prick.

Don't let the cross for you be in vain.[34]

Confess Jesus as Lord and be free in His Name.

Debbie Taylor

GOD'S PLAN

The devil planned a wicked trap.[35]

He thought from God's Word we had taken a nap.

But to his dismay he found us on guard

Anointed of God with myrrh and spikenard.

We are no longer living a life filled with sin.

We're no longer walking separated from Him.

We died on the cross crucified with our Savior[36]

Resurrected to live a life full of His favor.[37]

God's Word is a lamp and a light to our path.[38]

The devil's defeated that kindles his wrath.

Though he tempt us today with silver or gold

We'll not let this love for our Savior grow cold.[39]

Debbie Taylor

Our God releases our feet from the snare.[40]

Because He loved us, Jesus carried our care.

We carry no burdens. His yoke is so light![41]

Our lives are filled with the power of His might.[42]

We've escaped like a bird from the snare of the fowler.[43]

The devil is weak. He's a defeated prowler.

Our help is in the Name of the Lord.[44]

The anointing of Christ in our spirit's He's poured.

Freely we tell of our Father's great love.

With our eyes on Jesus we keep looking above.

We press toward the mark for the prize of high calling.[45]

We know from His love and His grace we're not falling.

Debbie Taylor

The ways of the Lord are loving and kind.

By the Spirit within us His Word we mind.

We're living in Him with His Word in our heart.[46]

He prospers and blesses each project we start.[47]

Our will and the Father's have become unified.

It's a oneness with God that will not be untied.

We know that we please Him as we walk in faith.[48]

To us He has multiplied His mercy and grace.

We're His bride, His temple, His body, His own.

We're the light of the world. We make His love known,[49]

To our neighbors, friends and those closest home.

We share God's goodness, how we're never alone.[50]

Debbie Taylor

Because of His love and His kindness to us,

In His powerful Word has grown a great trust

As the army of God we stand shoulder to shoulder

Like Jesus our Rock, we are strong as a boulder

We will win every battle as we stand together.

We'll not be shaken – whatever the weather.

By our Father's redemption we are sister and brother.

We'll stand victorious as we help one another.

THE NEW YEAR

You're more than a conqueror[51]

You're more than enough.

You're courageous and strong

You've got the right stuff.

No matter what comes no matter what stays

The Good Shepherd leads you in all the right ways.

God knows your thoughts & the intents of your heart.[52]

Stay on the straight path to the end from the start.

To begin may be small and the gate may be slim,

But the path grows quite bright as you walk close to Him.

Walk in the light of the Lord Who's within.

Stay clean from the world not entangled with sin.

Debbie Taylor

You're a vessel of honor[53]

For noble purpose.

Keep your heart pure

And stay free from the curses.

There's a new year ahead

More goals to be met.

Keep your eyes on the Lord

And the prize you will get.

This blessing I give you,

As one who does know.

Spend time in His presence

And let His grace flow.

Debbie Taylor

May His face shine upon you,

May God heap up in store

Great blessings and honors

As you walk through this door.

It's the power of choice

That you hold in your tongue

'Twill determine your victory

And the song to be sung.

It's been a good year of serving the Lord,

But there's more ahead great gifts to afford.

As we work together, our goal in plain view,

Our children will profit, we'll earn reward too.

Debbie Taylor

SCRIPTURE REFERENCES

1. Psalm 139:10
2. Ephesians 4:27
3. John 7:38*
4. Galatians 5:16
5. I John 3:2
6. I Thessalonians 4:17
7. Hebrews 4:11
8. Philippians 4:13
9. Deuteronomy 28:6
10. John 14:3
11. Romans 5:17, 21
12. Luke 9:1
13. Matthew 10:30
14. Proverbs 10:24
15. Jeremiah 33:3
16. Psalm 145:14
17. I Corinthians 15:57
18. Revelation 13:8
19. I Corinthians 15:45
20. John 10:10
21. Proverbs 6:31
22. Romans 10:14
23. Romans 10:17
24. Acts 14:3
25. Romans 10:9
26. I John 1:9
27. Colossians 3:3
28. Romans 3:14
29. Ephesians 4:12
30. I John 2:8
31. Corinthians 5:17
32. Luke 4:18
33. Mark 16:17
34. I John 5:12
35. II Corinthians 2:11
36. Galatians 2:20
37. Romans 6:4
38. Psalm 119:105
39. John 14:23
40. Psalm 91:3
41. Matthew 11:30
42. Ephesians 6:10
43. Psalm 124:7
44. Psalm 124:8
45. Philippians 4:13
46. John 15:7
47. Psalm 1:3
48. Hebrews 11:6
49. Matthew 5:14

Debbie Taylor

SCRIPTURES CONTINUED

50. Hebrews 13:5
51. Romans 8:37
52. Psalm 139:2
53. II Timothy 2:21

ABOUT THE AUTHOR

Debra Taylor grew up in New Orleans, Louisiana and was raised in the Greek Orthodox Church.

At sixteen she was born again and filled with the Holy Spirit. She began serving the Lord by teaching truths of the Bible that God revealed to her by His Spirit.

She now lives in Oklahoma with her husband, Nick, of thirty-seven years.

God has blessed them with four children who all help in the family business. They are raising families of their own and are all serving the Lord.

"I hope you enjoy these poems and that the reading of them will encourage and inspire you to fulfill the purpose that our gracious loving God has for you."

Debbie

Jeremiah 29:11

21140228R00027